Little Hen, Mouse, and Rabbit

Retold by Beverley Randell
Illustrations by Isabel Lowe

Little Hen, Mouse, and Rabbit
lived in a house by the woods.
Little Hen did all the work
in the house.

Mouse and Rabbit
sat on their chairs
all day long.
They were lazy!

One morning,
Little Hen went upstairs
to make the beds.

Mouse and Rabbit
were asleep
on their chairs.

The door was open,
and a hungry fox
came in.

Fox pushed Mouse
and Rabbit
into his bag,
and tied it up.

Fox ran off into the woods.

His bag was heavy.

He put it down

on the ground.

Then he went to sleep

under a tree.

Little Hen came downstairs.

Mouse was not there!

Rabbit was gone, too!

She ran into the woods

to look for them.

Little Hen saw Fox,
and she saw the bag.

A tail was coming out
of a hole in the bag!

Little Hen opened the bag,
and Mouse and Rabbit
climbed out.

They helped Little Hen
put some stones
inside the bag.
Then they tied it up again.

Little Hen and her two friends
ran back to their house.
They locked the door.

Fox woke up
and set off for home.
He had to cross a river
to get there.

But now his bag
was very heavy.
It was so heavy
that Fox fell down.
He fell into the river,
and that was the end of him!

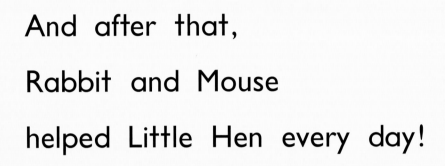

And after that,

Rabbit and Mouse

helped Little Hen every day!